NIC BISHOP
BUTTERFLIES

P9-CFU-918

Written and photographed by
Nic Bishop

SCHOLASTIC INC.
New York   Toronto   London   Auckland
Sydney   Mexico City   New Delhi   Hong Kong

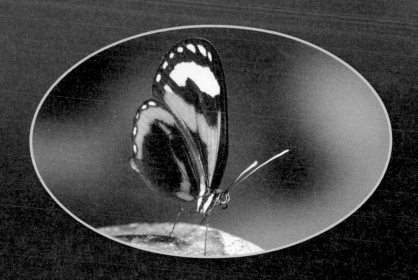

Butterflies are the most beautiful insects. Some have blue wings. Some have orange wings.

A few butterflies have wings you can see through.

The life of a butterfly starts with an
egg, which *hatches* into a caterpillar.

After it hatches, a caterpillar may eat
its eggshell.

There are many kinds of caterpillars. Some look scary. Some poke out stinky horns at enemies.

Caterpillars love to eat plants.
They eat and grow quickly. Soon, a
caterpillar grows too big for its skin.

Then it *molts*. The old skin splits open. The caterpillar wriggles out in a brand-new skin.

The hungry caterpillar keeps on eating. As it grows, the caterpillar will molt again. It may even eat its old skin!

In a few weeks, a caterpillar may be three thousand times bigger than when it hatched. Now the plump caterpillar finds a safe place.

It wriggles out of its skin one last time. Then it turns into a *pupa*. The pupa barely moves, day after day. But inside, the caterpillar's body is becoming a butterfly.

One day, the pupa splits and a
butterfly crawls out.

It stretches its brand-new wings.
It checks out its brand-new body.

A butterfly has big eyes to see the colors and shapes of flowers.

It can taste with its feet and smell with its *antennae*.

But best of all, butterflies can fly.
They skip and dance in the air.
It is hard for birds to catch them.

Butterflies love to visit flowers.
When one lands, it uncurls a long
tongue, like a drinking straw.
It drinks a sweet juice called
nectar from the flower. Nectar
is food for butterflies.

When some butterflies close their
wings, they can hide like leaves.

Other butterflies do not need to hide.
The colorful wings of a monarch butterfly
warn enemies that it tastes bad.

When a female butterfly is ready, she looks for the right place to lay her eggs. She will find plants her caterpillars love to eat.

There, she lays her eggs, so there will always be more butterflies.

A Closer Look with Nic Bishop

Butterflies are amazing insects. They dance through the woods and glide over fields. They can be found nearby in parks and backyards. Some live far away in rain forests. But no matter where they are, butterflies always catch your eye.

Taking photographs of butterflies and caterpillars is hard work. I traveled to South and Central America to find some of the butterflies in this book. I raised other butterflies at home. I waited for days to take pictures of eggs as they hatched. Sometimes I even waited for weeks! In the end, seeing the caterpillars turn into butterflies was worth every minute.

Glossary

antennae: moveable parts found on the heads of insects and used to sense things

hatch: to break out of an egg

molt: to shed an outer layer of skin

nectar: a sweet drink made by flowers that butterflies use for food

pupa: the stage of life between being a caterpillar and being a butterfly; also called a chrysalis

Photo Index

zebra longwing
butterfly, page 1

blue morpho butterfly,
page 2, front cover

longwing butterfly,
page 3 (top)

glasswing butterfly,
page 3 (bottom)

young monarch
caterpillar, pages 4, 5

spicebush swallowtail
caterpillar, page 6

black swallowtail
caterpillar, page 7

monarch caterpillar,
pages 8, 9, 10, 11, 12, 32,
back cover

monarch pupa,
page 13

monarch butterfly,
pages 15, 22–23

pipevine swallowtail
butterfly, page 16

peacock butterfly,
pages 18–19, 20

hairstreak butterfly,
page 21

leaf butterfly,
page 22

cabbage white butterfly,
page 25

butterfly eggs,
page 26

tiger swallowtail
butterfly, page 27

ISBN 978-0-545-28434-9

12 11 10 9 8 7 6 5 4   12 13 14 15 16/0

Printed in the U.S.A.   40

First printing, January 2011